A New Song on St. Paddy's Day

Emelda Ndive Powell

BOOK 2:
Music copy write page. All copy right reserved: @ No part of this music should not
to be reproduced with out the permission or authorization of the author.

E.Powell and the members of the university of NewHaven, WestHaven, CT, USA.
Internet: www.emeldapowellpca.com
C-Span 2
Library of Congress
Publishers
Author: E. Powell
Title: A New Song about St. Paddy.

Includes: 8 verses with various key notes to be song on St. Paddy's Day, March 17 every year. There is an
Editorial Page, Title page, all copy page highlighting page and references from other musicians worldwide.
Printed and Published in USA.

InfusedMedia Co. LLC
www.infusedmedia.co
1-888-251-6088

Author expresses the interest viewed and played in the music world from all ethnic groups.

Author opens with this expounding quotation of hers in music.

Oh! Music oh! Music bring me joy:" what does it mean? It means music can make the individual happy and glared into the aestic. World of Reality. Music strengthens, unite the racial population of the past, present and future of our societies." Oh music oh music brings Men joy".

Author owes much to many musicians worldwide like, J. Crowly and Associate. Impressive new Irish traditional group based on Waterford, sold millions of copies. American musicians also have British, his panic musicians, French, Italian, Russians, Spanish and Churches of all dominions have influenced the author so much. Author decided to write a new song on St. Paddy's, Jewish and all other middle East musicians have also influenced me greatly. Hope all will enjoy this master peace of St. Paddy's new song to be added to talent musician word wide.

Many thanks to the Board members of University of New Haven, CT. Member of Yale Violinist and all the contributors towards this research. Author was born in Cameroon, and raised in London, England, now living in USA as an American Citizen.

The University of New Haven

New Song of St. Patrick

By the supervision of Professor O'Conner, Dr.
Leiberman, Professor DePalmer and Professor Bablaw.

A Song for St. Patrick's Day

Emelda Powell

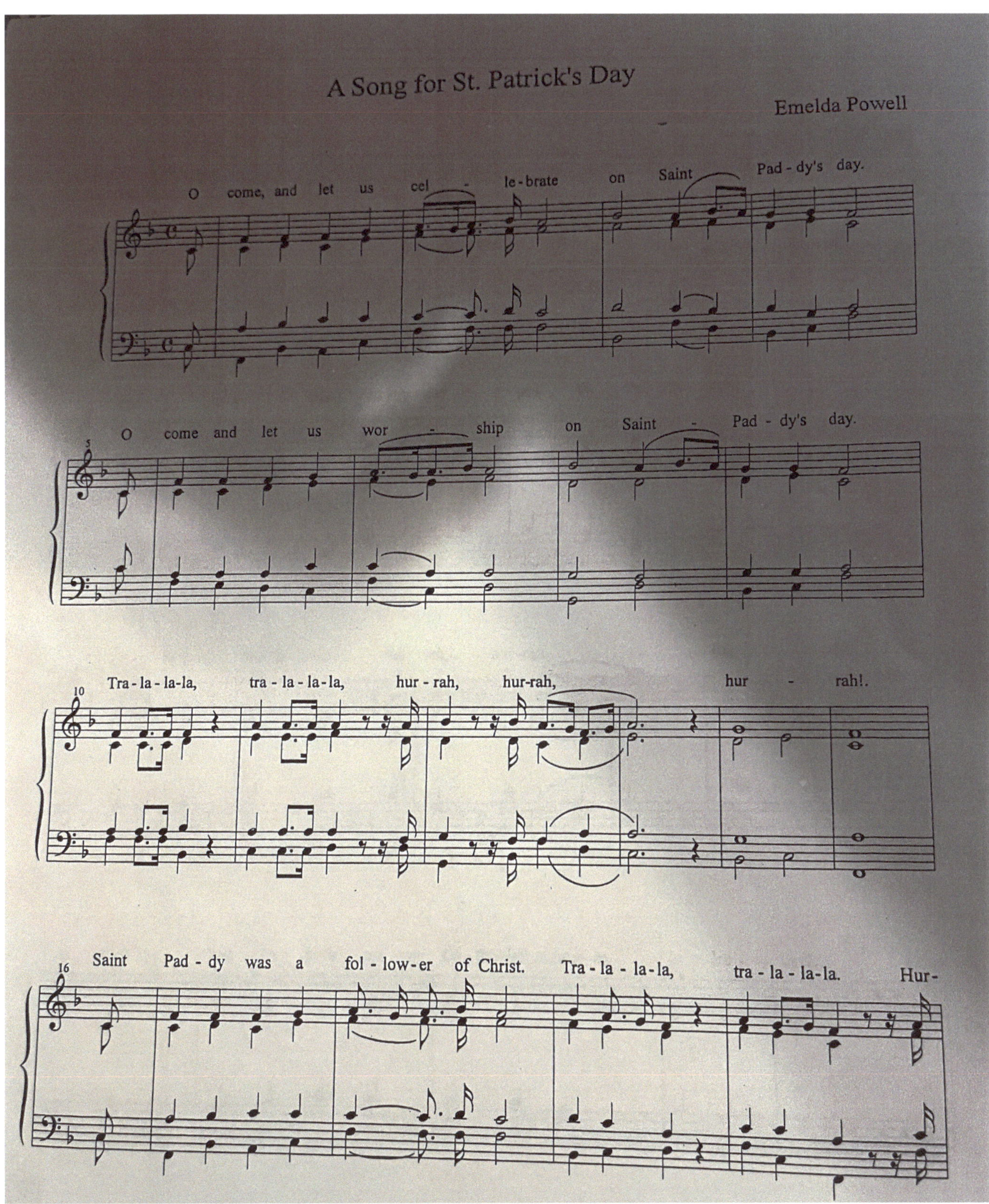

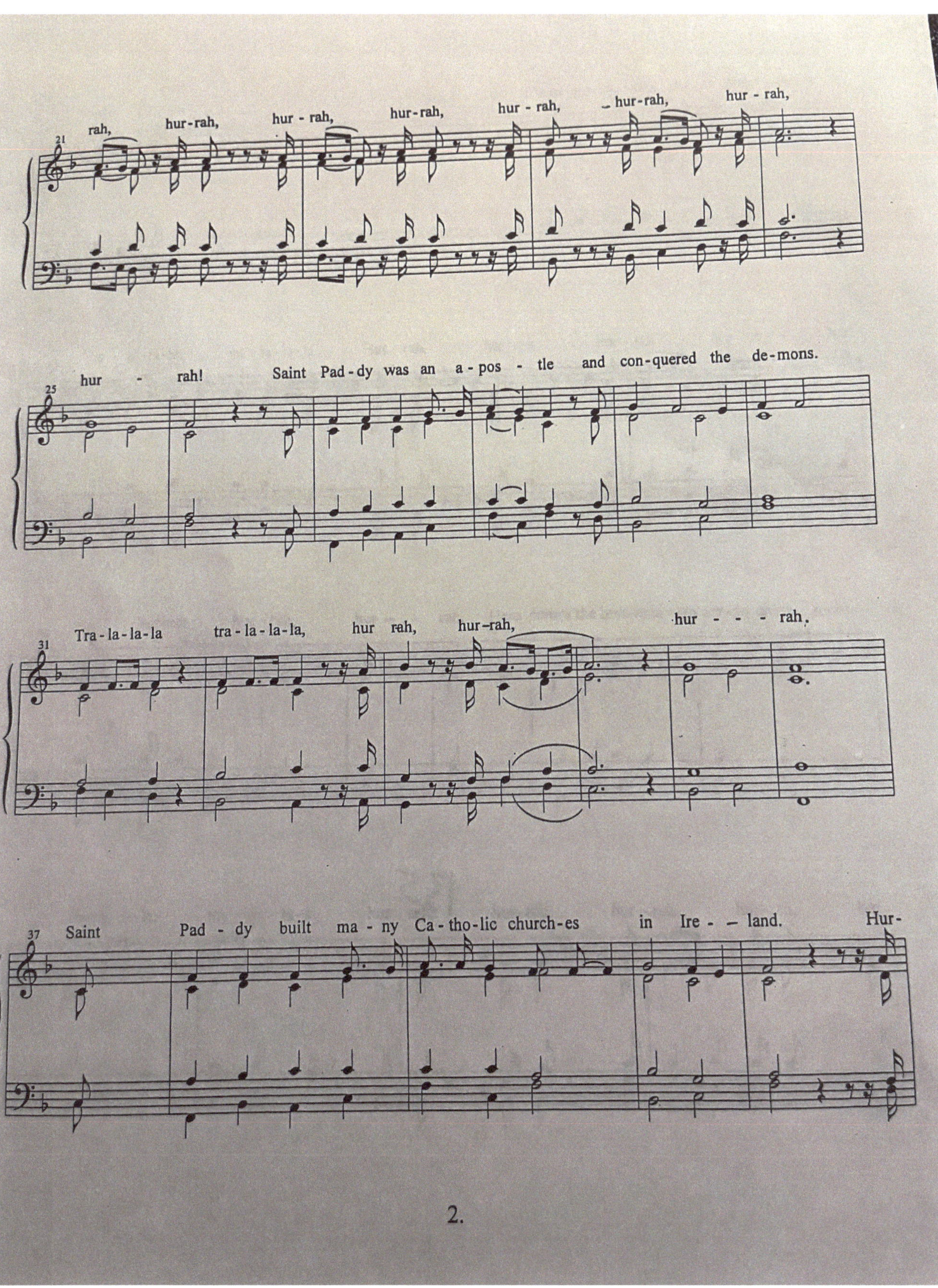
rah, hur-rah, hur-rah, hur-rah, hur-rah, hur-rah, hur-rah,
hur - rah! Saint Pad-dy was an a-pos-tle and con-quered the de-mons.
Tra-la-la-la tra-la-la-la, hur rah, hur-rah, hur - - - rah.
Saint Pad-dy built ma-ny Ca-tho-lic church-es in Ire—land. Hur-

2.

rah, hur-rah, hur - rah! Here comes a priest with ma-ny sham - rocks.
Tra - la-la-la, tra-la-la-la. Hur rah, hur-rah, hur-rah - hur-rah, hur-
rah, hur-rah, hur-rah, hur - - rah. Here comes the boat-man with ma-ny sham - rocks.
Tra-la-la-la, tra - la - la - la, hur rah, hur-rah, hur - rah, hur-rah, hur-

3.

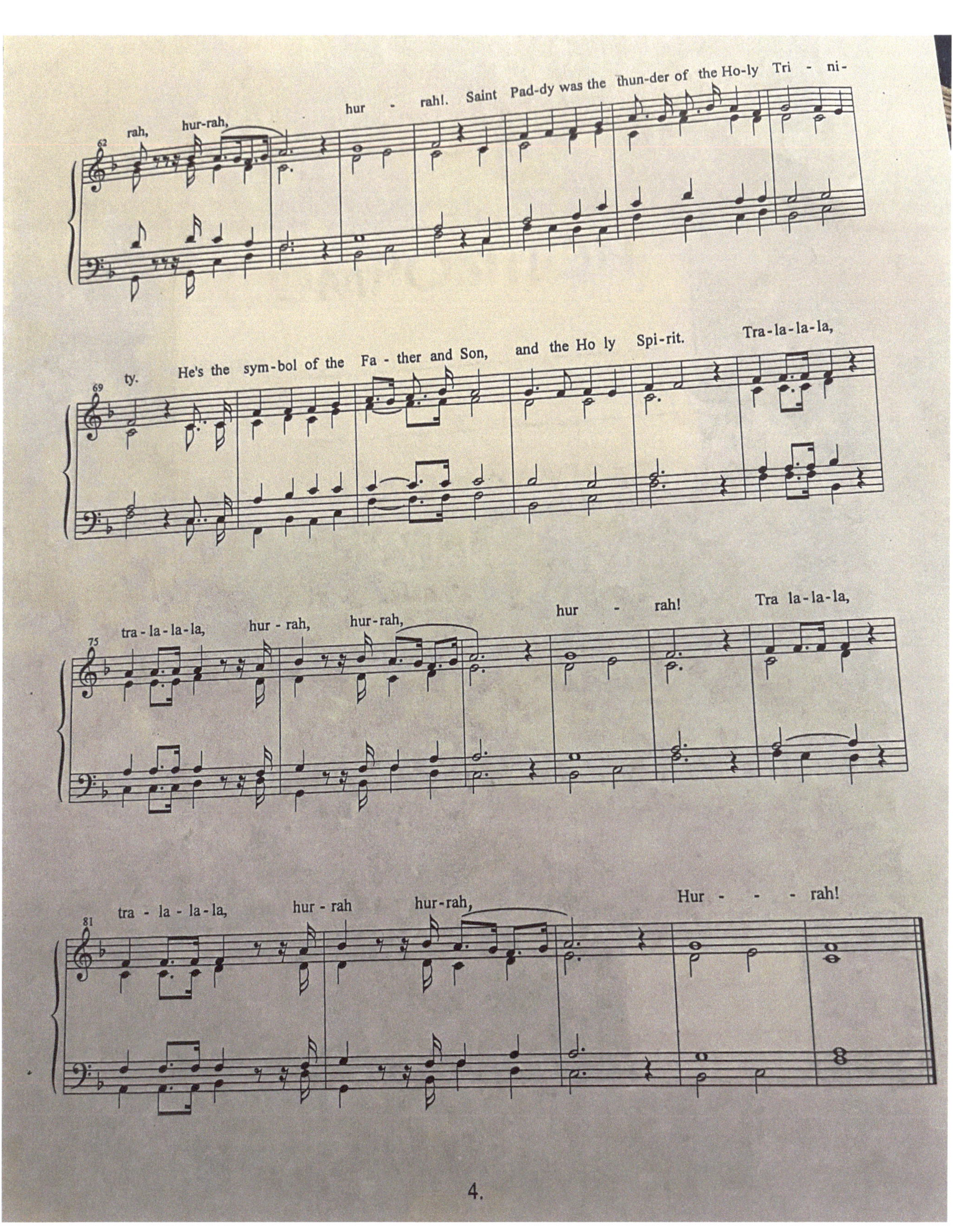

rah, hur-rah, hur - rah!. Saint Pad-dy was the thun-der of the Ho-ly Tri - ni-
ty. He's the sym-bol of the Fa - ther and Son, and the Ho ly Spi -rit. Tra-la-la-la,
tra - la-la-la, hur - rah, hur-rah, hur - rah! Tra la-la-la,
tra - la-la-la, hur - rah hur-rah, Hur - - - rah!

4.

"A New Song on St. Paddy's Day" by E. Powell.

"American Musicians of all Races" by Kenny Rogers, (Country Music) and (the blues in USA)

"Anao Atad" top traditional group from Corwall Bolingay Troy and Band.

"Celtic Cross" in England, High Energy from Lancaster, England.

"Merenge" by Kito.

West Indian Musicians, "Buffalo Soldier's by Bob Marley.

Celtic Musician, (Whales & England): Emma Christian, Manx Gaelic singe recorder player.)

Rita Connolly, (Irish Singer best known for her work on Granuaile, and other Davey pieces.)

Douglas Gurn, (Recorder playe composer, and much else: a specialist in Baroque music with a great twist on the music of O'Carolan Hispanic Musician: "La Tortura" by Shakira

Robin Huw Bowen, (the top player of the Welsh Triple Harp)

Cran, (Excellent and rising Irish traditional group)

Jimmy Crowley, (Inimitable and long-famed folk singer from Cork)

Andrea Bocelli, "The Prayer"

"Opera" by Pavarotti.

Irish Tenor: John Mcdermott, Anthony Kears, Findar Wright